MW00892609

Antique Dolls

Brenda Sneathen Mattox

DOVER PUBLICATIONS, INC.
Mineola, New York

INTRODUCTION

Whether you are a doll collector or hobbyist, or simply find the appeal of a well-made doll irresistible, you will find Brenda Sneathen Mattox's crisp, clear renderings an inspiration to color. Her artistry has captured the lively beauty of these antique dolls of the 19th and early 20th centuries. Represented on these pages are the French companies of Jumeau, Gaultier, Steiner, and Bru, as well as the German manufacturers Simon and Halbig, Kestner, and Kämmer and Reinhardt.

The French Jumeau dolls are among the most desired of all antique dolls. Pierre François Jumeau founded his company in Paris in 1842. A son, Emile, took over the company after his father's retirement. Under Emile's direction, a child-like doll was developed, in contrast to the more traditional "lady" doll. These new dolls, known as "Bébés," had bisque (unglazed china, a strong, natural-looking material) heads that could be turned from side to side, and fully jointed "composition" bodies made of materials such as paper, wood chips or pulp, and glue molded together to form body parts. Some Jumeau dolls had features such as pierced ears, a wig made of real hair or mohair, and moving "paperweight" eyes made of paperweight-type blown glass. Sizes ranged between 10 and 32 inches tall. Jumeau dolls were awarded numerous prizes in international competitions from the 1840s to the 1880s.

Many dolls produced in the second half of the 19th century had as much attention paid to their clothing as to their manufacture. The growth of the fashion industry in the 1860s and 1870s prompted dollmakers to compete in offering the latest in dress styles and hairdos. A painstakingly handmade lined silk or finely woven wool dress was a typical feature of these European dolls; hand-stitched pleating and correctly constructed undergarments were quite common as well.

Many antique dolls can be found today in private collections; others are on view in museums. There are many books available on the subject, as well as doll societies and clubs. Hopefully, this book will inspire you to seek out other sources regarding these precious, expressive creations, beloved and appreciated by so many.

NOTE: Without actual markings indicating when and by whom a doll was made, and in the absence of price tags, packing boxes, or original advertisements or catalogs, the origin of a particular doll can only be guessed. In addition, many dolls were made of parts from different manufacturers. When available, the name of the manufacturer/date of manufacture is given in this book. Some dolls are "in the style of" a particular manufacturer but cannot be authenticated.

Copyright

Copyright © 2000 by Dover Publications, Inc.
All rights reserved under Pan American and International Copyright Conventions.

Published in Canada by General Publishing Company, Ltd., 30 Lesmill Road, Don Mills, Toronto, Ontario.

Bibliographical Note

Antique Dolls is a new work, first published by Dover Publications, Inc., in 2000.

DOVER *Pictorial Archive* SERIES

This book belongs to the Dover Pictorial Archive Series. You may use the designs and illustrations for graphics and crafts applications, free and without special permission, provided that you include no more than four in the same publication or project. (For permission for additional use, please write to Permissions Department, Dover Publications, Inc., 31 East 2nd Street, Mineola, N.Y. 11501.)

However, republication or reproduction of any illustration by any other graphic service, whether it be in a book or in any other design resource, is strictly prohibited.

International Standard Book Number: 0-486-41318-7

Manufactured in the United States of America
Dover Publications, Inc., 31 East 2nd Street, Mineola, N.Y. 11501

Portrait doll, Jumeau, ca. 1860s.
Portrait painting, popular in the early 19th century,
influenced dollmakers in Europe.

Jumeau, ca. 1880s.
Note the painstakingly detailed eyelashes, a common feature
of French and German dolls of the time.

Jumeau, ca. 1890s.
Many Jumeau dolls were displayed in a variety of activities,
such as knitting, eating chocolate, conducting music,
reading a book, or playing an upright piano.

Jumeau, ca. 1900s.

"Long-faced" Jumeau.
Known in French as "Jumeau Triste" [sad], this type of doll
appeared in the 1870s and 1880s. The name refers to
the doll's serious, thoughtful expression.

Bru-type doll, ca. 1860s.

Bru lady doll, ca. 1870s.
"Kissing" and "whistling" Bru dolls were two of
the innovations of this French company.

"Black Bru," ca. 1890s.
Before the 1900s, an "ethnic" doll was typically a
standard head tinted to a darker skin color. Faces
occasionally were modeled more accurately.

François Gaultier-type lady doll, ca. 1870s.
The "lady" doll was often distinguished by its
narrow waistline and rounded bosom.

Bisque, François Gaultier, ca. 1880s.

French bride and groom, ca. 1850s.
These dolls were constructed of papier-mâché.
They are dressed in silk and wool costumes.

"Princess Alice" poured wax doll by Madame Montanari, ca. 1855.
Dollmaker Augusta Montanari produced dolls of the royal family;
this doll is believed to represent Queen Victoria's third child, Alice.

French lady doll, ca. 1865.

Bisque-head lady doll
with molded collar, ca. 1870.

French fashion doll, bisque, ca. 1870s.
Used to display fashions of the times, these dolls
were "dressed" by specialty craftsmen such as
lacemakers, wigmakers, and even jewelers.

French fashion bride, ca. 1870s.

French walking doll, ca. 1880.
These dolls had mechanisms that enabled them to "walk."
Some dolls were designed so that the head moved as the doll walked.

Bisque "Googly" doll, ca. 1900s.
"Googly" or "goo-goo" eyes lent this type of doll an impish expression.
The German dollmaker Armand Marseille produced many "goo-goos."

Simon & Halbig, ca. 1890s.
This German firm produced a high-quality
satiny finish to the bisque.

Standing doll: Simon & Halbig;
seated doll: Kestner. Ca. 1900s.

"Flirting Eye" doll, Simon & Halbig, ca. 1910.
A mechanism suspended the doll's eyes on a wire
held in place by string tied to holes in the head.

"Elise," Kämmer & Reinhardt "character" doll, ca. 1900s.
A character doll expresses individuality. Some character dolls are based on
an actual person; others embody a personality as envisioned by the designer.

Kämmer & Reinhardt, ca. 1920s.
This company operated the largest doll factory in
Germany. It later merged with Simon & Halbig.

Bisque, Steiner, ca. 1860.

Steiner, ca. 1890.

German china doll, ca. 1840s.
It is possible that this is a portrait doll of the
great German ballerina Fanny Elssler.

China lady doll, German, 1887.

Kestner, ca. 1900s.
J. D. Kestner produced highly prized bisque dolls.

Child: German, ca. 1880s;
mother: German, ca. 1860s.

Left: China-head lady doll;
right: untinted bisque, possibly C. F. Kling & Co.